GREAT AFRICAN AMERICANS IN
CIVIL RIGHTS

PAT REDIGER

Crabtree Publishing Company

Dedication

This series is dedicated to the African-American men and women who dared to follow their dreams. With courage, faith, and hard work, they overcame obstacles in their lives and went on to excel in their fields. They fought for civil rights and encouraged hope and self-reliance. They celebrated the glory of the athlete and the joy of knowledge and learning. They brought entertainment, poetry, and song to the world, and we are richer for it. *Outstanding African Americans* is both an acknowledgement of and a tribute to these people.

Project Manager
Amanda Woodrow

Writing Team
Karen Dudley
Pat Rediger

Editor
Virginia Mainprize

Research
Karen Dudley

Design and layout
Warren Clark
Karen Dudley

Photograph Credits
Jack T. Franklin Collection, courtesy of the Afro-American Historical and Cultural Museum: pages 18, 42; **Reuters/Bettman:** page 13; **UPI/Bettman:** pages 12, 14, 21, 25, 29, 35, 43, 44, 52, 61; **Blackstar:** pages 8 (Haun), 17, 20, 22, 26, 27 (Schulke), 24, 39 (Fitch), 31 (Johnson), 36 (Moore), 40 (Launois); **Canapress Photo Service:** pages 6, 28, 30, 37, 58; **Library of Congress:** pages 23 (GA-61-ATLA, 48-3), 45 (LC-U9-11696-15A); **Retna Ltd.:** page 16 (Granitz); **Schomburg Center for Black Research, The New York Public Library, Astor, Lenox and Tilden Foundations:** pages 32, 34, 38, 41, 55; **Urban Archives, Temple University:** pages 4, 5, 7, 9, 19, 46; **Woodfin Camp & Associates:** pages 10, 11, 15 (Downing), 33 (Ficara), 49 (Thomson).

Published by
Crabtree Publishing Company

350 Fifth Avenue,
Suite 3308
New York, New York
U.S.A. 10018

360 York Road, R.R. 4
Niagara-on-the-Lake,
Ontario Canada
L0S 1J0

73 Lime Walk
Headington
Oxford Ox3 7AD
United Kingdom

Cataloging-in-Publication Data

Rediger, Pat, 1966-
    Great African American in Civil Rights/by Pat Rediger.
    p. cm. — (Outstanding African Americans series)
    Includes index.
    Summary: Profiles notable African Americans in the field of civil rights including Martin Luther King, Jr., Malcolm X, and Marian Wright Edelman.
    ISBN 0-86505-798-2 (lib. bdg.)— ISBN 0-86505-812-1 (pbk.)
    1. Afro-American civil rights workers—Biography. 2. Civil rights movements United States—History—20th century. 3. Afro-Americans—Civil rights. 4. Afro-Americans. Social conditions. I.Title. II. Series: Rediger, Pat, 1966- Outstanding African Americans series.
    E747.R43 1995
    323'.092'273—dc20
    [B]

95-24881
                                                              CIP

Contents

Ralph David Abernathy

Personality Profile

Career: Clergyman, leader of the 1960s civil rights movement.

Born: March 11, 1926, in Linden, Alabama, to William and Louivery Abernathy.

Died: April 17, 1990, in Atlanta, Georgia.

Family: Married Juanita Odessa Jones, 1952. Had four children, Juandalynn Ralpheda, Donzaleigh Avis, Ralph David III, and Kwame Luthuli.

Education: Linden Academy; B.S., Alabama State College, 1950; M.A. in sociology, Atlanta University, 1951.

Awards: Peace Medal, German Democratic Republic (East Germany), 1971; numerous honorary degrees including LL.D.s from Allen University, 1960, Southampton College and Long Island University, 1969, Alabama State University, 1974; and D.D.s from Morehouse College, 1971, and Kalamazoo College, 1978.

Growing Up

Ralph was raised on a 500-acre farm near Linden, Alabama. The farm provided enough food and money for the family's comfort. Ralph was the tenth of twelve children. His parents named him David, but his sister nicknamed him Ralph after one of her favorite teachers, and the name stuck.

Both blacks and whites respected the Abernathy family because of Ralph's father, William. A strong believer in education and the church, William was a member of the local black school board and a church deacon. He gave generously of his time and money to both church and school.

From an early age, Ralph too was interested in religion. By the time he was seven, he knew that he would be a preacher when he was older.

After graduating from high school, Ralph was drafted into the U.S. Army and served during the final months of World War II. When the war ended, Ralph enrolled at Alabama State College in Montgomery. A popular student, he was elected president of the student council. Ralph organized student protests for better cafeteria food and places to stay. Ralph earned the respect of school officials, and, two years before graduating, he was hired as dean of men. Throughout his college years, Ralph was active in the church. In 1948, Ralph announced his calling as a Baptist minister.

Ralph's skill in preaching went beyond the Baptist ministry and helped him in the struggle for civil rights for African Americans.

Shortly after Ralph was born, his grandmother predicted that, one day, he would be known throughout the world.

Developing Skills

In 1950, Ralph enrolled at Atlanta University to study sociology. It was here that Ralph first heard Martin Luther King, Jr. preach. Impressed with Martin's learning and style, Ralph made friends with the young preacher. A few years later, both men were called to be preachers in Montgomery, Alabama, and soon Ralph became Martin's closest friend and advisor.

In 1955, Rosa Parks took her now-famous bus ride in Montgomery. At that time, Ralph and Martin had been talking a lot about civil rights. When Rosa was arrested for sitting in a white person's seat, they decided to form the Montgomery Improvement Association (MIA) to show support for her. The MIA persuaded African Americans to protest and stop using the bus line. The association organized carpools and the city's black taxi cabs to take people where they needed to go. The boycott was a success, and, in 1956, the U.S. Supreme Court ended separate seating.

Ralph outside the headquarters of the Southern Christian Leadership Conference in Atlanta in 1970.

In 1957, Ralph and Martin formed the Southern Christian Leadership Conference (SCLC), a group of churches and organizations that pushed for civil rights in a nonviolent fashion. Ralph was the secretary-treasurer.

Four years later, Ralph moved to Atlanta with Martin and became pastor of the West Hunter Street Baptist Church. The two men walked in marches, staged sit-ins, and led rallies across the South in support of civil rights. When Martin was assassinated in 1968, Ralph was by his side.

After Martin's death, Ralph was elected SCLC leader. He continued to organize many demonstrations including the Poor People's Campaign which wanted better conditions for low-income and unemployed Americans.

Ralph led the SCLC until 1977. He went on to form the Foundation for Economic Enterprises Development (FEED) to train African Americans so they could find better jobs. Ralph continued as a minister at West Hunter Street Baptist Church in Atlanta until his death on April 17, 1990.

After Martin Luther King, Jr.'s death in 1968, Ralph was elected leader of the SCLC, a position he held until 1977.

"As we were standing together one day,…[my father] said, 'David, if you ever see a good fight, get in it – and win it.'"

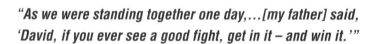

Accomplishments

1948 Announced his calling as a Baptist minister.

1951 Pastor of the First Baptist Church in Montgomery.

1955 Co-founder of the Montgomery Improvement Association.

1957 Co-founder of the Southern Christian Leadership Conference (SCLC).

1961 Pastor of the West Hunter Street Baptist Church in Atlanta.

1968 SCLC president, led the Poor People's Campaign and Resurrection City.

1972 Participated in World Peace Council in Santiago, Chile.

1977 Resigned as SCLC president, became president emeritus.

1989 Published autobiography, *And the Walls Came Tumbling Down*.

Overcoming Obstacles

As a civil rights leader, Ralph was in constant danger. He and his family received many threats from white racists who did not want African Americans to have equal rights. He was arrested many times for organizing marches and sit-ins to protest unfair laws against black people. Shortly after the SCLC was formed, Ralph's home and church were bombed. Ralph was in Atlanta when the bomb went off, but his family was at home and barely escaped. Ralph quickly returned to Montgomery to rebuild his home and church.

Ralph ran into trouble with the government during his Poor People's Campaign. He led a group of demonstrators to Washington, D.C. They built a shantytown near the center of the city and called their village Resurrection City. Ralph met with members of Congress to ask for more help for the country's poor people. Congress did not want to deal with Ralph, so they waited for the time when his demonstration permit would run out and his group would have to leave. When Ralph told everyone to stay, he was arrested.

Ralph attended Dr. Martin Luther King, Jr.'s funeral in 1968.

Some people in the civil rights movement felt Ralph was crude. He said what he felt and did not seem to care if he hurt people's feelings. These critics preferred the style of Martin Luther King, Jr. who was more cultured. But many agree that the movement needed Ralph as well as Martin. They were a good team. While Martin appealed to the people in the cities, Ralph was more popular with country people because of his rural background.

During the 1970s and 1980s, Ralph faded from the civil rights movement. Younger leaders who were not so aggressive began to take over. Ralph turned to other activities. He ran for the U.S. Congress but received only five percent of the vote. Ralph believed that most of his supporters wanted him to stay in the civil rights movement instead of being a congressman.

Ralph spent part of his final years lecturing across the country. He developed heart problems and began to tour less often. In his last years, he spent most of his time looking after his church in Atlanta.

Ralph at the Poor People's March in 1968.

In 1989, Ralph published his autobiography, *And the Walls Came Tumbling Down*. The book contained some criticisms of Martin Luther King, Jr. Some people felt those comments about Martin should have been left out. But others supported Ralph. They said a good autobiography should not censor the bad, and the bad was well-known anyway. Ralph's book is now widely recognized as a fascinating record of the civil rights movement.

Special Interests

- Ralph's reputation as a champion of peace and equality went well beyond the United States. He received the Peace Medal from the German Democratic Republic (East Germany) in 1971. Ralph was also a participant in the World Peace Council meeting in Santiago, Chile, in 1972.
- Ralph was also a good writer. Many of those involved in the civil rights movement felt his autobiography captured the spirit of those times.

Marian Wright Edelman

Education: Marlboro Training High School; studied in France and Switzerland, 1958-59; B.A., Spelman College, 1960; LL.B., Yale University Law School, 1963.

Awards: Outstanding Leadership Award of the National Alliance of Black School Educators, 1979; Distinguished Service Award of the National Association of Black Women Attorneys, 1979; National Award of Merit of the National Council on Crime and Delinquency, 1979; Washingtonian of the Year, 1979; National Women's Political Caucus/Black Caucus Outstanding Leadership Achievement Award, 1980; Rockefeller Public Service Award, 1981; Gertrude Zimand Award, National Child Labor Committee, 1982; Roy Wilkins Civil Rights Award, NAACP, 1984; A. Philip Randolph Award, the National Urban Coalition, 1987; the Albert Schweitzer Humanitarian Prize, Johns Hopkins University, 1988.

Personality Profile

Career: Lawyer and founder of the Children's Defense Fund.

Born: June 6, 1939, in Bennettsville, South Carolina, to Arthur and Maggie Wright.

Family: Married Peter Edelman, 1968. Has three children, Joshua Robert, Jonah Martin, and Ezra Benjamin.

Growing Up

Marian's father, Arthur, was a Baptist minister who believed African Americans had to help each other. Since blacks were not allowed in public parks in his neighborhood, he helped build a park and roller skating rink behind his church. He also set up the Wright Home for the Aged. Arthur impressed upon Marian the importance of hard work. She spent long hours at school and also volunteered for church and community activities.

Arthur believed that if Marian saw successful African Americans, she would work as hard as they did. Whenever important black people lectured in town, Arthur made sure his children heard them. Marian is actually named after Marian Anderson, a famous black opera singer her father once heard.

Marian graduated from Marlboro Training High School before attending Spelman College, a school for African-American women in Atlanta, Georgia. Marian's marks were so high that she received several grants to study and travel in Europe. She was a student in France and Switzerland for a year and also toured Russia for two months.

"The message of my racially segregated childhood was clear: let no man or woman look down on you, and look down on no man or woman."

Developing Skills

Marian returned from Europe to continue her studies. But her travels had changed her. She had seen blacks living as equals in other countries. Back in the South, she heard the words of civil rights leaders such as Martin Luther King, Jr., and she became active in the civil rights movement. She participated in the largest sit-in in Atlanta to protest unfair laws against African Americans. When she and thirteen other students were arrested, Marian realized that African Americans needed civil rights lawyers if things were going to change.

In 1960, Marian enrolled at Yale University Law School. During her spring break, she went to Mississippi to help blacks register to vote. It was a dangerous task. White racists threatened black people who tried to get their names on the voters' lists.

After graduating from law school in 1963, Marian joined the National Association for the Advancement of Colored People (NAACP) in Jackson, Mississippi. A year later, she opened her own law office in Jackson and became the first black woman to pass the Mississippi bar exam. She worked to free black students who had been jailed for protesting against unfair treatment of African Americans.

Marian also became involved with the Head Start program for children. She could see that poverty was a fact of life for many black children. They suffered because their parents had lost their jobs when new machines replaced them in the cotton fields.

At age twenty-nine, Marian moved to Washington, D.C., to start the Washington Research Project. The organization suggests changes to laws in order to help lower-income people. Marian saw how much children suffered from poverty, and she felt someone had to speak on their behalf. In 1973, Marian founded the Children's Defense Fund (CDF), a non-profit group that helps children. Based on the belief that it is more difficult to help people after they are adults, the CDF urges the government to help people while they are still young.

Marian is in constant demand as a speaker. She has written several books. One of her books, *The Measure of Our Success*, became a bestseller.

Marian with President Bill Clinton following her presentation at an economics conference in late 1992.

Accomplishments

1963 Graduated from Yale University's Law School.

1964 Opened her own law office in Jackson, Mississippi.

1964-68 Headed NAACP Legal Defense and Education Fund in Mississippi.

1965 First black woman to pass the bar exam in Mississippi.

1973 Founded the Washington Children's Defense Fund.

1980 First black and second woman to chair the board of trustees at Spelman College.

1985 Awarded the MacArthur Foundation Prize fellowship.

1992 Published *The Measure of Our Success*.

Overcoming Obstacles

W hen Marian was a lawyer in Mississippi in the 1960s, her work often put her in danger. White racists did not want her to represent blacks, and she was threatened by dogs and thrown in jail. Even though she was a lawyer, she was not allowed inside the Mississippi state courthouse. Many of her clients came out of jail with broken bones or missing teeth. One of them was even shot while in jail. Marian sometimes wondered if being a lawyer would really change things, but she realized that if she could handle these problems, she could handle anything.

In 1967, Marian took Senator Robert Kennedy and his assistants on a tour of the slums of the Mississippi Delta. She showed them where families lived without heat, light, or running water. During this tour she met Peter Edelman, one of Robert's assistants. The two became close friends and married a year later.

The poverty in Mississippi and the assassination of Robert Kennedy and Martin Luther King, Jr. convinced Marian that she had to do more for the civil rights movement. She was upset that government programs to help lower-income people were often cut. Marian realized that if she wanted to change things in Mississippi, she would have to start by changing things in Washington. Marian applied for and received a grant to study how people suffering from poverty could be helped by changing the laws.

As CDF president, Marian has addressed many of these problems. The CDF has become the nation's most active and effective organization involved with children and family issues. Its programs encourage children to stay in school and warn them of the problem of teenage pregnancy.

Marian has accomplished a great deal as CDF president, but she still finds time to be a wife and mother of three children. In the early 1970s, Marian was still working in Washington when her family moved to Boston. She continued to work in the capital but flew home every weekend to spend time with her family. Marian and her family moved back to Washington in 1979.

In recognition of her hard work and determination, Senator Edward Kennedy once called Marian "the 101st Senator on children's issues."

Marian spoke to Harvard graduates in 1991.

Special Interests

- Marian likes to read in her spare time — even if she has to do it in the bathtub! She enjoys non-fiction, but sometimes reads fiction by Robert Ludlum and Helen MacInnes.
- To relax, Marian listens to music, plays the piano, or works in her garden.
- She likes to find new art work to add to her collection.

Coretta Scott King

Personality Profile

Career: Civil rights activist, author, and singer.

Born: April 27, 1929, in Heiberger, Alabama, to Obadiah (Obie) and Bernice Scott.

Family: Married Martin Luther King, Jr., 1953. Has four children, Yolanda Denise, Martin Luther III, Dexter Scott, and Bernice Albertine.

Education: A.B., Antioch College, 1951; Mus.B., New England Conservatory, 1954.

Awards: National Council on Negro Women Annual Brotherhood Award, 1957; Louise Waterman Wise Award, 1963; Myrtle Wreath Award, Cleveland Hadassah, 1965; Wateler Peace Prize, 1968; Dag Hammerskjøld Award, 1969; Pacem in Terris award, International Overseas Service Foundation, 1969; Premi Antonio Feltrinelli for exceptional display of high moral valor, 1969; Leadership for Freedom Award, Roosevelt University, 1971; Martin Luther King Memorial Medal, College of the City of New York, 1971; Eugene V. Debs Award, 1982; numerous honorary degrees.

Growing Up

On April 27, 1929, Coretta was born in a small house on her grandfather's farm in Alabama. Her father was one of the hardest working people in the neighborhood, and he taught his children to be the same. Coretta and her sister looked after the farm's garden and crops. Money was scarce for the Scott family. When she was ten, Coretta earned money for school supplies by picking cotton in the fields.

Coretta's parents believed that education was the first step towards freedom. Even before Coretta began school, her mother read stories to her. When Coretta started going to school, she had to walk three miles there and back.

Coretta enjoyed school, especially her music classes. She was asked to lead the songs whenever the county supervisor came to inspect the school. Later, at Lincoln High School, Coretta learned to read music and play different musical instruments. When she graduated, she won a partial scholarship. Coretta went to Antioch College in Ohio, following her older sister, who had been the first black student to attend.

At college, Coretta continued to study music. Her singing voice was quite lovely, and she sang in many concerts and recitals. She even appeared on the same program as the world-famous baritone Paul Robeson. Coretta also studied elementary education and hoped to be a teacher. She was the first black woman at Antioch College to major in education.

"When I was very young and growing up, I was protected from the extreme hardships of segregation though I was always aware of being deprived of the rights to which I was ontitlod."

Developing Skills

While Coretta was at Antioch College, her professors encouraged her to continue her music studies. Coretta took their advice and followed her dream. She enrolled in advanced music training at the New England Conservatory in Boston. It was here that she met Martin Luther King, Jr. Two years later, on June 18, 1953, the couple was married.

The year after her wedding, Coretta completed her master's degree in voice. Although she was still interested in music, she had found a new purpose. Coretta now spent much of her time helping her husband in the civil rights movement.

At first, Coretta was by Martin's side at every meeting and rally. Later, as Martin became more involved in civil rights activities, Coretta also became busier. She often went to meetings as Martin's representative and made speeches on his behalf. She was also active in the peace organization Women's Strike for Peace. In 1962, Coretta was a delegate at the Disarmament Conference in Geneva, Switzerland.

Coretta with Martin Luther King, Jr. on the Selma to Montgomery march in 1965.

In spite of her busy life, Coretta managed to keep up with her music. She taught voice lessons at Morris Brown College in Atlanta. She also organized concerts to raise money for the civil rights and peace movements.

After Martin was assassinated, Coretta became the new leader of the civil rights struggle. She led demonstrations and founded the Martin Luther King, Jr. Center for Nonviolent Social Change. The center's work is to preserve Martin's dream and continue his work.

Through Coretta's efforts, the neighborhood where Martin was born was declared a National Historic Site. In 1984, Coretta was elected chairperson of the Martin Luther King Holiday Commission. The commission worked to have the third Monday in January made a national holiday in honor of Martin.

Coretta shaking hands with a well-wisher as she leaves after speaking at the National Education Association's Human Rights Awards dinner in 1969.

Accomplishments

1948 Performed as a professional singer in Springfield, Ohio.

1960 Attended White House Conference on Children and Youth.

1962 Protested as a member of the Women's Strike for Peace group against nuclear weapons in Geneva, Switzerland; became voice instructor at Morris Brown College in Atlanta, Georgia.

1969 Founded the Martin Luther King, Jr. Center for Nonviolent Social Change Inc. in Atlanta, Georgia.

1980 Became commentator for the Cable News Network.

1984 Elected chairperson of the Martin Luther King Holiday Commission.

Overcoming Obstacles

Coretta first became aware of racism when she was a child growing up in Alabama. She had to enter the local white-owned drugstore by the side door and then wait until all the white children were served. While white children were bussed to their own school, Coretta had to walk three miles to an all-black school.

Schools for blacks were not so well-equipped as other schools were. Coretta's school did not even have a library. By the time Coretta got to college, she had a lot of catching up to do. The other students had come from better schools and had better educations. Coretta had to study very hard. She even took a remedial reading class. Despite these obstacles, Coretta did quite well in school.

Coretta also experienced racism when she was at Antioch College. The college required its education students to teach in the public schools for a year. The school board refused to let Coretta teach in their schools because she was black. She responded by becoming more active in civil rights.

In 1976, Coretta and her family attended a ceremony honoring Martin Luther King, Jr.'s birthday.

As Coretta and Martin got more involved in the civil rights movement, they started to receive death threats. People threw bricks through their windows and made harassing phone calls to them. In 1956, their home was bombed.

The bombing scared Coretta. For the first time, she realized that she and her family could be killed. Instead of backing away, Coretta became even more active in the civil rights movement.

In 1968, Coretta's fears were realized when Martin was assassinated in Memphis, Tennessee. Again, Coretta did not back away. Four days after his murder, she led a huge rally at the site of his death. Even through her grief, she urged all Americans to seek a peaceful society rather than revenge. This march was just the first of many that Coretta would lead. Two months later, she marched in the Poor People's Campaign to protest against unfair treatment of lower-income people.

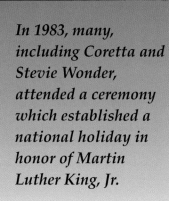

In 1983, many, including Coretta and Stevie Wonder, attended a ceremony which established a national holiday in honor of Martin Luther King, Jr.

Coretta has kept alive Martin's dream of an equal, peaceful society. She has received many honors and awards for her work. She has also been awarded over 100 honorary doctoral degrees.

Special Interests

- Coretta has always been interested in music. When she moved to Atlanta, she became a music instructor at Morris Brown College. She also performed as a singer at Freedom Concerts.
- Coretta is a great speaker and also a superb administrator. When Martin operated his office out of their home, she handled most of her husband's mail and phone calls.

Martin Luther King, Jr.

Family: Married Coretta Scott, 1953. Had four children, Yolanda Denise, Martin Luther III, Dexter Scott, and Bernice Albertine.

Education: B.A., Morehouse College, 1948; S.D., Crozer Theological Seminary, 1951; Ph.D., Boston University, 1955; D.D., Chicago Theological Seminary, 1957; D.D., Boston University, 1959.

Awards: Received numerous awards including the Spingarn Medal from the NAACP, 1957; Anisfield Wolf Award, 1958; Man of the Year, *Time* magazine, 1963; Nobel Peace Prize, 1964; Judaism and World Peace Award from Synagogue Council of America, 1965; Brotherhood Award, 1967; Nehru Award for International Understanding, 1968; Presidential Medal of Freedom, 1977.

Personality Profile

Career: Baptist minister, founder of the Southern Christian Leadership Conference, and civil rights leader.

Born: January 15, 1929, in Atlanta, Georgia, to Martin, Sr. and Alberta King.

Died: Assassinated on April 4, 1968, in Memphis, Tennessee.

Growing Up

Baptist ministers seemed to run in the King family. Martin's grandfather and father were Baptist ministers. Both served as the pastor of the Ebenezer Baptist Church in Atlanta, Georgia. Although the King family was better off than most African Americans, they experienced racism and unfair treatment.

Martin's father wanted his son to follow in his footsteps. But Martin was not sure. He felt the church would not be a suitable place to talk about racism. A college professor told Martin that the ministry was an important career and could be used as a place to fight racism. This convinced Martin to become a minister.

This is the house in Atlanta, Georgia, where Martin was raised.

Martin studied at the Crozer Theological Seminary in Chester, Pennsylvania, from 1948 to 1951. He was elected student president and graduated at the top of his class. He received a grant to continue his studies and decided to attend Boston University.

Martin graduated when he was twenty-five and was offered several jobs. He felt it was his duty to return to the South and try to improve life for African Americans. He became the pastor of the Dexter Avenue Baptist Church in Montgomery, Alabama. His first year was very busy. He worked hard to meet the needs of his new congregation. It was here that he first showed signs of becoming a great speaker.

"[Martin] was mature beyond his years; he spoke as a man who should have had ten years more experience."

Developing Skills

I n 1955, Martin and other black leaders formed the Montgomery Improvement Association (MIA). He was elected president. The MIA supported Rosa Parks, a black woman who was arrested and fined for not giving up her bus seat to a white person. They encouraged Rosa to take her case to the U.S. Supreme Court. Martin and other MIA leaders saw this as an opportunity to unite the people of Montgomery to protest against unfair laws against African Americans. The MIA instructed all African Americans in the community to boycott the bus line and demanded that bus drivers treat black passengers with respect on a first-come, first-served basis. When the courts changed the law, Martin and Rosa were the first African Americans to board the bus.

Since the MIA was so successful, Martin decided to expand his activities. At age twenty-eight, Martin formed the Southern Christian Leadership Conference (SCLC) to fight for civil rights. Martin traveled across the country and in one year made 208 speeches. Since Martin was so busy, he resigned from his church in Montgomery and took a part-time position with his father at the Ebenezer Baptist Church in Atlanta.

Martin in his office in 1963. A portrait of Indian civil rights leader Gandhi hangs on the wall. He was a great influence on Martin.

In 1963, Martin led demonstrations in Birmingham, Alabama, to convince the city to employ blacks in better jobs and to end segregation in stores. He was arrested and placed in solitary confinement. There he wrote "Letter from a Birmingham Jail," one of the most important documents of the civil rights movement.

Martin's most famous speech, "I Have a Dream," took place during the 1963 March on Washington. Two hundred and fifty thousand people marched to the nation's capital to mark the 100th anniversary of the ending of slavery.

On April 4, 1968, Martin spoke at a rally in Memphis, Tennessee, to help striking sanitation workers improve their working conditions. The next day, while standing on the balcony of the Lorraine Motel, he was shot. He was buried in South View Cemetery in Atlanta. Later his body was moved to the Martin Luther King, Jr. Center for Nonviolent Social Change in Atlanta.

Martin with the Nobel Peace Prize he won in 1964.

Accomplishments

1948 Ordained Baptist minister.

1954 Pastor of the Dexter Avenue Baptist Church in Montgomery, Alabama.

1955 President of the Montgomery Improvement Association. Played a leadership role in the local bus boycott.

1957 Co-founded the Southern Christian Leadership Conference in Atlanta.

1960 Co-pastor at the Ebenezer Baptist Church in Atlanta.

1963 Organized protests in Birmingham, Alabama. Wrote "Letter from a Birmingham Jail." Delivered historic "I Have a Dream" speech during March on Washington Campaign.

1964 Awarded Nobel Peace Prize.

1965 Organized protests in Selma, Alabama, which eventually gained new voting rights for blacks in that state.

1966 Launched campaign to end segregation in Chicago, Illinois.

Overcoming Obstacles

Martin has become a symbol for the civil rights movement. There are monuments and honors in his name across the country. Martin's success did not come easily. He and his family were constantly in jeopardy. After telling people not to use the bus in Montgomery, Martin was arrested. He received hate mail and phone threats, and his house was bombed.

When Martin organized a protest march in Birmingham, Alabama, the police used clubs and dogs against the protesters. The state court ruled there would be no more protests, but Martin disobeyed the court. He was thrown into jail. There he wrote "Letter from a Birmingham Jail" which told his supporters to fight for civil rights without using violence.

After Martin was released, he led another protest. The police used violent force to stop the protesters. People all over the country saw the action on television and were shocked. The government of the United States was forced to pass new laws giving equal treatment to all African Americans.

Martin realized many angry whites wanted to kill him. In his speeches, Martin sometimes mentioned the possibility of being killed. But he kept preaching that the struggle for freedom must be nonviolent.

Martin strongly believed in using nonviolent methods to achieve equality for African Americans.

Martin was criticized by other people in the civil rights movement. Some did not agree with Martin about nonviolence. Sometimes his closest advisors disagreed with him. Leaders of other civil rights organizations also questioned his leadership.

There were many failures along the road to winning equal treatment for blacks in America. Martin wanted to end racist laws not only in the South, but in the North as well. But many people in the northern cities, especially in the black ghettos, did not believe in Martin's nonviolent ways. They believed that only violence would achieve their goals. This gave rise to a new movement called Black Power. It became popular in Chicago, Los Angeles, Boston, and Philadelphia. Riots broke out, and Martin continued to plead for nonviolence. In 1964, Martin was awarded the Nobel Peace Prize, the most important prize in the world given to those who work for peace.

Martin with one of his daughters in 1964.

Special Interests

- Martin liked to write. He wrote for many publications, contributed to several anthologies, and authored several books.
- Martin was very interested in promoting education for African Americans. He was a member of the Baptist Teaching Union Congress and the National Sunday School.
- Although Martin was very busy, he loved spending time with his four children.

Thurgood Marshall

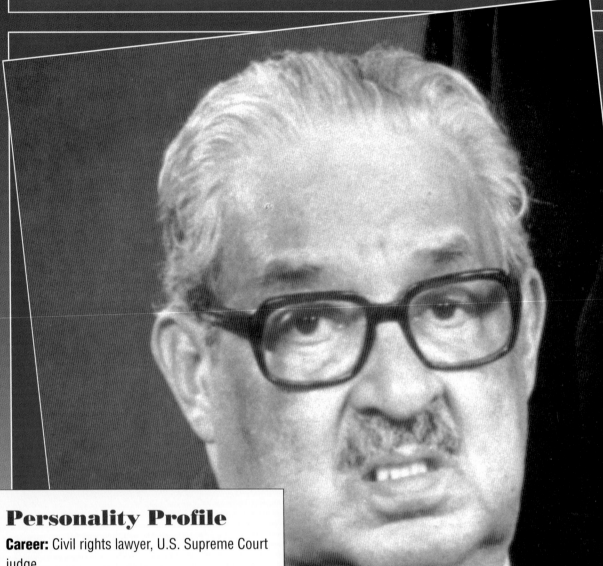

Personality Profile

Career: Civil rights lawyer, U.S. Supreme Court judge.

Born: July 2, 1908, in Baltimore, Maryland, to William and Norma Marshall.

Died: January 24, 1993, in Bethesda, Maryland.

Family: Married Vivian Burey, 1929, (died in 1955); married Cecilia A. Suyat, 1955. Had two sons, Thurgood, Jr. and John William.

Education: B.A., Lincoln University, 1930; LL.B., Howard University Law School, 1933.

Awards: Spingarn Medal from NAACP, 1946; Horatio Alger Award from Horatio Alger Association of Distinguished Americans; numerous honorary degrees.

Growing Up

Thurgood was born in 1908, in Baltimore, Maryland, to parents who taught him to be proud of his ancestry. The family traced its roots to a nineteenth-century slave who had caused so much trouble that his owner set him free. Thurgood's parents taught their son to stand up for himself, and if someone made a racist comment to him, he was to fight back.

Thurgood's father believed that crime and poverty came directly from laziness. In order to avoid this fate, Thurgood was enrolled at the school where his mother taught so she could keep an eye on him. But Thurgood was a prankster who enjoyed being the class clown. Unfortunately, the teachers did not like his jokes. As punishment they made him read the United States Constitution out loud. He knew it by heart by the time he finished high school.

When Thurgood was NAACP Head Special Counsel, he often argued cases before the Supreme Court.

Thurgood's parents urged him to get the best education he could. In 1925, he enrolled at Lincoln University, near Philadelphia, Pennsylvania. His mother sold her engagement ring to help pay for his school expenses. At first, she tried to persuade Thurgood to become a dentist, but he was more interested in law. He soon transferred to Howard University, an all-black law school in Washington, D.C. At age twenty-five, Thurgood graduated at the top of his class. He passed the Maryland bar exam later that year.

"We lived on a respectable street, but behind us there were back alleys where the roughnecks and the tough kids hung out. When it was time for dinner, my mother used to go to the front door and call my older brother. Then she'd go to the back door and call me."

Developing Skills

T hurgood set up his own law office in Baltimore. Many of his first cases were for the National Association for the Advancement of Colored People (NAACP). His first case for the NAACP involved the University of Maryland which had refused to let a black student attend its all-white law school. Thurgood won the case, bringing him to the attention of the NAACP's national office. In 1936, he was invited to become an assistant special counsel, and, two years later, he became the head special counsel.

Thurgood with his wife and children on his first day at work as justice of the Supreme Court in 1967.

Thurgood developed his skills as a lawyer with the NAACP. He traveled across the country fighting for civil rights. Thurgood found that his high school punishments had paid off. His major weapon in these civil rights cases was his knowledge and use of the Constitution.

Thurgood represented black students who wanted to attend white universities, and he fought for blacks to serve on juries.

Thurgood's biggest case occurred in 1954. He led a team of lawyers that was opposed to separate schooling for blacks and whites, a practice that had been going on for fifty years. The case went all the way to the U.S. Supreme Court. After winning, Thurgood was nicknamed "Mr. Civil Rights."

Thurgood had wanted to be a judge, but he had not believed that his dream would be possible because of his color. With the end of segregated schooling and the civil rights movement in full swing, Thurgood decided to try to become a judge.

Many politicians were against his decision. But in 1961, Thurgood was appointed a judge. Four years later, he became the U.S. Solicitor General, a position in which he represented the government in Supreme Court cases. His most important case at this time led to the adoption of the Miranda Rule, which requires police to read suspects their rights.

Thurgood worked hard as Solicitor General, and, in 1967, he was appointed to the U.S. Supreme Court by President Lyndon Johnson. As a Supreme Court justice, Thurgood's decisions reflected his commitment to the civil rights movement. After a long, successful career, Thurgood resigned in 1991.

Thurgood was a Supreme Court Justice from 1967 until his retirement in 1991.

Accomplishments

1933 Opened private law practice in Baltimore, Maryland.

1936 Assistant special counsel to the National Association for the Advancement of Colored People (NAACP).

1940 Became director of legal defence and education fund for the NAACP.

1961 Named judge for the Second Circuit Court of Appeals.

1965 Named U.S. Solicitor General.

1967 Appointed to the U.S. Supreme Court.

Rosa Parks

Personality Profile

Career: Seamstress, civil rights worker.

Born: February 4, 1913, in Tuskegee, Alabama, to James and Leona McCauley.

Family: Married Raymond Parks, 1932, (died 1977).

Education: Montgomery Industrial School for Girls.

Awards: Southern Christian Leadership Conference named Rosa Parks Freedom Award in her honor, 1963; Spingarn Medal, NAACP, 1979; Martin Luther King, Jr. Award, 1980; Service Award, *Ebony*, 1980; Martin Luther King, Jr. Nonviolent Peace Prize, 1980; Eleanor Roosevelt Women of Courage Award, Wonder Woman Foundation, 1984; Martin Luther King, Jr. Leadership Award, 1987; many honorary degrees.

Growing Up

Rosa sat at the front of the bus after the historic Supreme Court ruling which banned bus segregation in 1965.

Rosa spent most of her early years on her grandparents' farm near Pine Level, Alabama. She lived with her mother, grandparents, and younger brother. The farm was a scary place to live. The Ku Klux Klan, a group of whites who believe they are superior to blacks, burned farms and hanged blacks. Rosa's grandfather slept with a shotgun to protect the family.

As a child, Rosa worked at a nearby plantation picking corn, peanuts, and potatoes. Back then, black children often worked in the fields. Their school even closed three months earlier than the white school so they could work all day.

Rosa's first school was a small shack, and the students had few textbooks. They had to take their books home at night for fear the Ku Klux Klan would steal them. Most students who graduated were qualified only for manual labor. Rosa's mother, Leona, wanted a better life for her daughter. When Rosa was eleven, her mother sent her to a much better private school in nearby Montgomery. Sometimes Rosa's mother had trouble coming up with the money for school fees, so Rosa cleaned and dusted the classrooms to help pay for her tuition.

When the private school closed, Rosa continued her education in public schools. She left in grade eleven to look after her grandmother and then her mother, both of whom had become ill. Rosa did not finish high school until after she was married.

"By the time I was six, I was old enough to realize that we were not actually free....I had a very strong sense of what was fair."

Developing Skills

After her mother recovered from her illness, Rosa returned to Montgomery and got a job making shirts. When she was in her late teens, Rosa met Raymond Parks. Impressed with both him and his work in civil rights, Rosa married Raymond in December, 1932. Together, Rosa and Raymond got involved with the National Association for the Advancement of Colored People (NAACP) and the Montgomery Voters' League. Both groups fought for civil rights, especially the right for black people to vote.

Rosa and Ralph Abernathy at the Ebenezer Baptist Church during the Montgomery Bus Boycott.

Rosa's greatest contribution to the civil rights movement took place on December 1, 1955. In those days, the Montgomery bus system had special rules for black people. They had to enter the bus by the front door, pay their fare, then leave and board by the back door. They could sit only at the back of the bus, while whites sat at the front. There was a middle section that blacks could use only if no white person was sitting there. On December 1, Rosa was sitting in this section when a white person boarded the bus. The whites-only section was filled, and the driver told Rosa to get up and stand at the back so the white passenger could sit in the middle section. Rosa refused. She was taken to the police station and placed in a jail cell.

Many black leaders were outraged by Rosa's arrest. They told other blacks to protest and not use the bus system. This boycott went into effect on December 5, 1955. The next day, Rosa was found guilty. She appealed the ruling and was released on bail.

The boycott lasted for 381 days until Rosa's case was decided in the U.S. Supreme Court. The judges ruled that blacks and whites could no longer be separated on the bus.

Rosa moved to Detroit, Michigan, to find a quieter life. She continued to make speeches and raise money for the NAACP. At age seventy-four, she founded a school for blacks in Detroit. It is called the Rosa and Raymond Parks Institute for Self Development.

In 1989, Rosa was honored at the NAACP's annual convention.

Accomplishments

1933 Held a variety of jobs, eventually becoming a seamstress at the Montgomery Fair Department Store.

1955 Refused to give up her bus seat to a white man. This action led to the historic Montgomery bus boycott.

1956 U.S. Supreme Court ruled that blacks and whites cannot be segregated on buses.

1957 Rosa, her husband, and mother moved to Detroit, Michigan.

1965-1988 Staff assistant to U.S. Congressman John Conyers.

1987 Founded the Rosa and Raymond Parks Institute for Self Development.

Overcoming Obstacles

Rosa's childhood was like that of many other African Americans. She went to an overcrowded and poorly equipped school. She could drink only at certain water fountains. She could not enjoy lunch at certain restaurants. Rosa learned to cope with these insults. She often protested against them in her own way. She would not use the public facilities marked "colored." Rosa took the stairs rather than the colored elevator. One day she walked through a white neighborhood. She was pushed from behind by a white boy, so Rosa pushed him back. The boy's mother asked Rosa how she dared to touch a white boy. Rosa said she did not want to be pushed by anyone.

Rosa protested against the bus company in many ways. She was once thrown off the bus for boarding by the front entrance. Sometimes she would just walk home.

On that famous day when she was arrested, it would have been much easier for Rosa to give up her seat. Three other black women who were sitting beside her did. She could have avoided being arrested, fingerprinted, and sent to jail. But Rosa was tired. Her back was sore from pressing pants all day at work, and she was tired of racism.

Even after she was arrested, Rosa could have accepted her fine. But she felt someone had to take a stand for civil rights. It was not an easy decision. She discussed it with her husband, mother, and a lawyer before going ahead.

Once Rosa decided to fight, she was in constant danger. Her family received death threats, and Rosa and her husband both lost their jobs. The strain was so great that her husband suffered a nervous breakdown. Even though Rosa won her court case, she and her family had to leave Montgomery because no one would hire them.

Rosa at Martin Luther King, Jr.'s funeral in 1968.

When she moved to Detroit, Rosa remained active in the civil rights struggle by making speeches and marching in demonstrations. Today, Rosa is recognized and honored as the "mother of the civil rights movement." In Detroit, a street and an arts center bear her name in celebration of her achievements.

Special Interests

- Rosa is working closely with the National Committee for the Rosa Parks Shrine. It will act as a library to house her personal papers.
- Since Rosa spent much of her early days caring for sick people in her family, she considered becoming a nurse.
- Rosa is a member of the African Methodist Episcopal Church, where she enjoys singing and praying. As a young person, she was a member of the Allen Christian Endeavor League.

Malcolm X

Personality Profile

Career: National Minister for the Nation of Islam, founder of Muslim Mosque, Inc. and the Organization of Afro-American Unity, and a human rights activist.

Born: May 19, 1925, in Omaha, Nebraska, to Earl and Louise Little.

Died: Assassinated February 21, 1965, in Harlem, New York.

Family: Married Betty, 1958. Had six daughters.

Education: Left school after grade eight.

Growing Up

Malcolm's father, the Reverend Earl Little, was a Baptist minister who believed blacks would never find peace in the United States. Instead, he thought they should return to Africa to lead a natural and peaceful life. Many whites did not like Earl's views. The Ku Klux Klan, a group that believes whites are a superior race, made terrifying visits to the house. They threatened to kill Earl and his family. One of Malcolm's earliest memories was of their house being burned to the ground. The fire department did nothing to put out the fire.

Earl was killed in 1931, and it was rumored he had been murdered by the Klan. Malcolm's mother, Louise, had difficulty looking after her many children, and the state welfare department constantly harassed her. She had a nervous breakdown and was sent to the state mental hospital when Malcolm was twelve years old.

Malcolm and his brothers and sisters were split up and sent to different foster homes. Malcolm turned to stealing because he was angry. He moved to Boston, Massachusetts, to live with his half-sister, Ella. She encouraged him to look for a job; instead, he found trouble. He became friends with gamblers and thieves and started selling illegal liquor and drugs. In 1946, Malcolm was sentenced to ten years in jail for stealing.

Malcolm in 1939 at age fourteen.

"Early in life, I had learned that if you want something, you had better make a noise."

"I felt a challenge to plan, and build, an organization that could help cure the black man in North America."

While in prison, Malcolm learned about the Nation of Islam (Black Muslims). This group preached that blacks are superior to whites. It wanted a section of the United States to separate and become a nation for blacks. Malcolm felt this religion answered many of his questions. He read and participated in debates and began preaching to other inmates.

Malcolm was released from jail when he was twenty-seven. He became the assistant minister in Muslim Temple Number One in Detroit, Michigan. He also changed his last name from Little to X. The X represented the African tribe he came from but did not know.

Malcolm quickly became well known in the Black Muslim community. The congregation loved his fiery sermons, and the leaders were impressed with his enthusiasm. Malcolm became the leading preacher for the Nation of Islam. He told African Americans to gain back their self-respect and urged them to use violence against white people because they had treated black people so unfairly.

In 1964, Malcolm changed his beliefs. He felt the Nation of Islam no longer answered his needs, so he turned to traditional Islam, visited its holy city of Mecca in Saudi Arabia, and changed his name to El-Hajj Malik El-Shabazz. Malcolm then established his own groups, Muslim Mosque, Inc. and the Organization of Afro-American Unity.

In 1964, Malcolm campaigned in Chester, Pennsylvania, to desegregate the public school system.

Malcolm traveled throughout the Middle East and Africa. He studied with other followers of the Islamic faith. He learned to cooperate with people of other races and to believe people should try to live together. When Malcolm returned to the United States, he said it was wrong to group all white people as racist.

Malcolm began preaching his new ideas. He received a number of death threats from his former followers who disagreed with his beliefs. In February, 1965, Malcolm delivered his last speech. While addressing a crowd in the Audubon Ballroom in Harlem, New York, he was shot and killed by three men.

Throughout the early 1960s, Malcolm addressed many people. He is shown here in 1963 at a Harlem rally.

Accomplishments

1952 Assistant minister for the Nation of Islam (Black Muslim) religious order. Changed name from Malcolm Little to Malcolm X.

1953 Established new temple in Boston.

1955 Established new temple in Philadelphia.

1964 Resigned from Nation of Islam and formed Muslim Mosque, Inc. and the Organization of Afro-American Unity. Made a pilgrimage to Mecca and changed name to El-Hajj Malik El-Shabazz.

Overcoming Obstacles

Malcolm was faced with obstacles his entire life. He was raised in the mid-West, where his family was constantly harassed by white supremacists. When he was only four years old, his house was destroyed in a fire. The incident convinced his parents to move to Lansing, Michigan, where they thought they would be out of the Klan's reach. When his father was killed and his mother was taken from him, Malcolm fended for himself in several foster homes. His teachers were not helpful. He once told an English teacher he wanted to be a lawyer, but the teacher told him that was impossible for a black person. He advised Malcolm to become a laborer.

In 1963, after Malcolm spoke at a Harlem rally, violence broke out in the crowd.

Malcolm became angry about the way he was treated and turned to drinking to overcome his troubles. He stole, gambled, and sold illegal drugs and liquor. Malcolm used hair straightening chemicals because he wanted to look like a white man. He believed if he looked white, he would be treated as a white.

Malcolm hit bottom when he went to jail in 1946. He decided to take this chance to improve his education and started reading. Malcolm felt white writers had underestimated what blacks had achieved and that his troubles were caused by white racists. He also learned about the Nation of Islam. It taught him that blacks were superior to whites, and he realized he should be proud of who he was.

The Nation of Islam was a big help to Malcolm. But the group later became his biggest obstacle. Many ministers were jealous of Malcolm's accomplishments. They lied about Malcolm to the leader, Elijah Mohammad. Malcolm's break with Elijah took place in 1963, when Malcolm made a comment about President John F. Kennedy's assassination that was taken the wrong way. Elijah suspended Malcolm for ninety days for the comment. Malcolm realized that Elijah had his own faults but was never punished for them.

Malcolm decided to form his own organization. This worried Nation of Islam ministers. They felt their members would join Malcolm's organization and told their members not to follow. Some angry ministers sent Malcolm death threats through the mail. Others phoned and threatened to kill him. Malcolm's house was firebombed on February 14, 1965. His wife, who was pregnant with twin girls, and his four daughters barely escaped injury. The three men who assassinated him a week later were members of the Nation of Islam. In 1966, these three men were convicted of Malcolm X's murder.

Malcolm with civil rights leader, Martin Luther King, Jr.

Special Interests

- Since his penmanship was poor, Malcolm decided to take steps to improve it. He opened a dictionary and wrote every word until his penmanship was superb.
- Malcolm took great pride in his appearance. He was always well-groomed and, after his early years, did not smoke or drink.

Dorothy Height

D orothy's early role models were her parents. They were busy in the church and volunteer organizations in Rankin, Pennsylvania. They encouraged Dorothy to play basketball and become a public speaker. Dorothy was an A student and applied to Barnard College. She was told to wait a term because the college accepted two African Americans a year, and those had already been accepted. She received a thousand-dollar scholarship for winning a national oratory contest and instead went to New York University, where she received a master's degree in psychology.

Dorothy had a keen interest in the problems black women faced.

Dorothy worked for two years at the New York City welfare department. In the evening, she studied at the New York School of Social Work. In 1937, Dorothy met Mary McLeod Bethune, president of the National Council of Negro Women (NCNW). This meeting sparked Dorothy's interest in the problems black women faced.

At age twenty-six, Dorothy joined the YWCA in New York City and became the assistant director of the YWCA's Emma Ransom House, a home in Harlem for black women. She worked to get fair wages for black domestic servants working in white homes.

In addition to her YWCA work, Dorothy remained interested in women's groups. One of her favorite groups was Delta Sigma Theta, a sorority for blacks. In 1947, she was elected president. During her ten years as president, she worked to increase the number of jobs for black women. She also helped improve the ties between African-American women and those in Third World countries. Dorothy increased the number of services to the sorority's members. In Georgia, for example, she developed a bookmobile program for black people.

In 1956, at age forty-four, Dorothy resigned from the YWCA to seek new goals. A year later, she became president of the National Council of Negro Women (NCNW). She used the position to help the civil rights movement and to improve the living conditions of many African Americans. During the 1960s, she organized members of the group to assist African Americans register to vote. She was the chief organizer behind "Operation Woman Power," a program that helped women start their own businesses and receive job training.

Personality Profile

Career: Leader of several women's organizations including the National Council of Negro Women.

Born: March 24, 1912, in Richmond, Virginia, to James and Fannie Height.

Education: B.A. and M.A. from New York University; postgraduate studies at the New York School of Social Work.

Awards: Distinguished Service Award, National Conference on Social Welfare, 1971; inducted into the International Women's Hall of Fame, 1991; honorary degrees from Tuskegee University, Coppin State College, Harvard University, and Pace College.

Dorothy was asked by the YWCA, the organization she had worked for, to help desegregate its branches. For years, the YWCA had black branches and white branches, but the two did not mix. Dorothy designed a plan to integrate them. Getting this plan to work, especially in the South, was not easy, but Dorothy helped to make the change as smooth as possible.

In the 1980s, Dorothy and the NCNW organized a series of "Black Family Reunion Celebrations" to promote black family life. She felt that if blacks took pride in their heritage, then such problems as drug use, delinquency, and teen pregnancy would decrease. These celebrations included seminars on family planning and health care. Young adults also learned about job opportunities.

Under Dorothy's direction, the NCNW got teenagers involved in working against drugs, school drop-out, and unemployment. By helping solve the problems of their community, teens would develop skills to help them in their own lives. Dorothy has earned many honors for her work. In 1991, she was inducted into the International Women's Hall of Fame.

Accomplishments

1944 Staff member of the YWCA national board in New York City.

1946 Named director of the YWCA Center for Racial Justice.

1947 Appointed president of the Delta Sigma Theta sorority.

1957 Named president of the National Council of Negro Women.

1991 Inducted into the International Women's Hall of Fame.

Jesse Jackson

Often the victim of racism, Jesse decided to overcome prejudice by trying to do the best he could.

J esse grew up in Greenville, South Carolina. His mother was an unwed, black teenager, and his father was a middle class, married man who lived next door. Often the victim of racism, Jesse decided to overcome prejudice by trying to do the best he could. He became president of his class, the honor society, and the student council. Jesse was also a member of the football, basketball, and baseball teams. But Jesse could not get away from racism. Although he was an excellent baseball player, he had no future in the game because he was black.

In 1959, Jesse left the South to attend the University of Illinois. He did not like the university. He was not allowed to play quarterback on the football team and could not attend local concerts because of his color. Jesse transferred to the North Carolina Agricultural and Technical College, a black college in Greensboro. Here he was the quarterback, an honor student, fraternity officer, and student body president. He also became interested in the civil rights movement. Jesse joined the local chapter of the Council on Racial Equality (CORE). He participated in sit-ins and organized protest rallies.

In 1968, Jesse was ordained a Baptist minister. While he was still studying to be a minister, Jesse joined Martin Luther King, Jr. and his civil rights organization, the Southern Christian Leadership Conference (SCLC), in protests in Alabama. He decided to commit himself totally to the civil rights movement.

Jesse moved to Chicago, Illinois, and became the national director of Operation Breadbasket, a program which encouraged white businesses to hire more African Americans. It also arranged for boycotts of those businesses that refused to do so.

Jesse became involved in other protests. He led marches of people suffering from hunger and unemployment on the Illinois state capital. The state responded by increasing funding for school lunch programs.

Personality Profile

Career: Civil rights leader, politician, founder of PUSH and the National Rainbow Coalition, Inc.

Born: October 8, 1941, in Greenville, South Carolina, to Noah Robinson and Helen Jackson.

Education: University of Illinois, 1959-60; B.A., North Carolina Agricultural and Technical College, 1964; Chicago Theological Seminary, 1964-66.

Awards: Rockefeller Grant, mid-1960s; Presidential Award, National Medical Association, 1969; Humanitarian Father of the Year, National Father's Day Committee, 1971; numerous honorary degrees from colleges and universities.

After Martin Luther King, Jr.'s death, Jesse became dissatisfied with the SCLC and often disagreed with its leaders. In 1971, he formed his own organization, People United to Save Humanity (PUSH).

In 1983, when he was forty-three, Jesse ran for the Democratic presidential nomination. He campaigned for new programs to help the poor. He did not win, but he received a lot of support and convinced Americans of all colors that an African American could become president. Jesse turned that support into a new organization, the National Rainbow Coalition. It was a group of people of many races dedicated to overcoming poverty.

Jesse moved to Washington, D.C., and was elected the District of Columbia's "statehood senator." He lobbied Congress to recognize the district as a separate state. He also became host of a television show, "Voices of America with Jesse Jackson."

Accomplishments

1964	Field representative for the Council on Racial Equality.
1966	Chicago coordinator of Operation Breadbasket.
1967	Named national coordinator of Operation Breadbasket.
1968	Ordained a Baptist minister.
1971	Founded People United to Save Humanity (PUSH).
1983	Candidate for Democratic presidential nomination.
1986	Founded the National Rainbow Coalition.
1988	Candidate for Democratic presidential nomination.
1989	Hosted "Voices of America with Jesse Jackson."
1991	Elected statehood senator for the District of Columbia.

Vernon E. Jordan, Jr.

Vernon was a talented speaker and won many prizes in oratory.

Vernon grew up in the deep South at a time when African Americans were treated as "equal, but separate." He could go only to a black school, drink from a blacks-only water fountain, and had to sit upstairs in theaters. Even his home, which was in one of the first public housing projects built only for blacks, was in a segregated area.

Vernon was an excellent student and basketball player. He entered DePauw University in Greencastle, Indiana, and studied political science, history, and speech. He acted in plays, one of which he wrote about racism in the South. Vernon was a talented speaker and won many prizes in oratory.

In 1957, Vernon graduated from college and enrolled in law at Howard University in Washington, D.C. When he graduated, Vernon was offered jobs in several large law firms in the capital, but he joined a firm in Atlanta, Georgia, because it specialized in civil rights. One of his most important cases involved representing a black woman who wanted to attend the University of Georgia. Vernon won the case against the university. On her first day of classes, he used his body to shield her from an angry crowd as she entered the campus.

At age twenty-seven, Vernon became the Georgia field secretary for the National Association for the Advancement of Colored People (NAACP). He made speeches, organized rallies, and called for boycotts of industries that would not hire blacks. Soon, a number of Atlanta stores were hiring blacks.

After two years, Vernon moved to Arkansas and started his own law firm. He also became director of the Voter Education Project, traveling across the South and registering African Americans to vote. Within four years, two million new black voters had been registered, and the number of black elected officials had increased eight times.

Personality Profile

Career: Civil rights lawyer, executive director of the United Negro College Fund, and former executive director of the National Urban League.

Born: August 15, 1935, in Atlanta, Georgia, to Vernon and Mary Belle Jordan.

Education: B.A., DePauw University, 1957; LLB, Howard University, 1960.

Awards: Fellowships to Harvard University's Institute of Politics, John F. Kennedy School of Government, Metropolitan Applied Research Center; Old Gold Goblet from DePauw University, 1969; honorary degrees from Brandeis University, Bloomfield College, Morris Brown College, and Wilberforce University.

Vernon became the executive director of the United Negro College Fund (UNCF) in 1970. The organization raised money for black colleges. One year, Vernon raised $8 million for thirty-six colleges.

When he was only thirty-six, Vernon was appointed the executive director of the National Urban League. This organization helped people living in city slums, many of whom were black. It raised money for job training and for educating children. The League had an annual budget of more than $100 million, much of which came from the U.S. government.

In 1980, Vernon was shot in the back after a National Urban League rally in Fort Wayne, Indiana. Vernon spent three months in the hospital and underwent six operations. The next year, Vernon resigned from the National Urban League, saying ten years as leader was long enough. The past few years had been hard for him. Government funding for the League had been cut, and many of Vernon's white allies felt that race was less of a problem than it had been. Vernon joined a law firm in Dallas, Texas, where he continued to defend civil rights cases.

Accomplishments

1962 Georgia field secretary for the National Association for the Advancement of Colored People.

1964 Established his own law firm and became director of the Voter Education Project.

1970 Executive director of the United Negro College Fund.

1971 Executive director of the National Urban League.

1981 Joined the Dallas, Texas, law firm of Akin, Gump, Strauss, Hauer & Feld.

Audley Moore

A udley was born in New Iberia, Louisiana, in 1898. When she was five, her mother died, and her father was unable to care for the family. He sent Audley and her two younger sisters to live with their grandmother. Even at this young age, Audley was aware of the racism and hatred in the South. She knew that her grandfather had been lynched by a white mob, and she watched helplessly as her grandmother's second husband also was lynched.

A few years later, Audley and her sisters joined their father in New Orleans. But the violence and prejudice towards blacks there was just as bad as it had been in New Iberia. Audley began to develop a strong sense of racial pride and a desire to fight racism.

Audley began to develop a strong sense of racial pride and a desire to fight racism.

Audley's father died when she was in grade four, and Audley had to leave school to support her sisters. By lying about her age, she managed to get a job as a hairdresser and earned enough money to take care of the family.

During World War I, Audley and her two sisters traveled to Anniston, Alabama, to help with the war effort. When they arrived and saw how poorly the black soldiers were treated, the three women organized the black community to provide food and supplies for the men.

Audley returned to New Orleans where she married and opened a store with her husband. In 1919, Audley attended a lecture by Marcus Garvey. Marcus told the crowd they should take pride in their heritage, and he called for the establishment of a black nation. Audley was delighted to find others who felt the same way she did, and she joined Marcus's group, the United Negro Improvement Association.

In 1922, Audley and her family moved to Harlem, New York, in search of a better life. Conditions there were as difficult as in the South. Black women workers were treated like slaves and were paid as little as fifteen cents a day. Audley started up the Harriet Tubman Association to help them fight for better wages and working conditions. She also joined the International Labor Defense and later the Communist Party.

Throughout the 1930s, Audley organized working-class people to fight racism and segregation. She helped get black baseball players accepted into the major leagues and fought against landlords who kicked out black tenants. She also organized rallies to protest rent increases.

Personality Profile

Career: An organizer for civil rights, women's rights, and Pan-African nationalism.

Born: 1898 in New Iberia, Louisiana, to Henry and St. Cyr Moore.

Awards: Named "Queen Mother" by the Ashanti people of Africa.

In the 1950s, Audley returned to Louisiana and launched a campaign demanding that the government pay African Americans $500 million for the hardships their ancestors had endured as slaves. This process is known as reparation. Audley wanted the money to help African Americans get an education and gain a sense of their cultural identity. Although her campaign was unsuccessful, Audley did not give up. She pursued her dream of teaching racial pride to blacks by organizing the African-American Cultural Foundation and founding the Eloise Moore College of African Studies.

For the next twenty years, Audley continued to set up many more organizations for African people. She often traveled to Africa, visiting heads of state and attending conferences. While in Ghana, she was named "Queen Mother" of the Ashanti people in honor of her lifetime work for civil and human rights.

Accomplishments

1919 Became interested in Pan Africanism after listening to Marcus Garvey (founder of the United Negro Improvement Association).

1933 Joined the Communist Party and organized protest rallies.

1955 Launched national crusade for reparations to African Americans.

1962 Organized the Reparations Committee of the Descendants of United States Slaves; filed an unsuccessful claim with a California court.

1970 Founding member of the Congress of African Peoples.

A. Philip Randolph

In 1889, Philip was born in Crescent City, Florida, to parents who taught him to be proud of his black heritage. Philip's father was a tailor and minister who thought that his son should also become a preacher, but Philip had other ideas. Philip dreamed of becoming a lawyer or politician. He wanted to be in a position of power so he could help in the fight for African-American civil rights.

Although Philip was a good student in high school, he did not have enough money to attend college. He moved to New York City where he worked at a number of odd jobs while attending night classes at City College.

It was at college that Philip met Chandler Owen. The two men began a magazine for black workers called *The Hotel Messenger* (later named *The Messenger*). In it they wrote about racial justice and urged African Americans to arm themselves against the violence of white racist mobs. They also criticized the U.S. involvement in World War I. By 1919, the U.S. Attorney General had named Philip "the most dangerous Negro in America."

Philip began to get more involved with black workers and the labor movement. At that time, many labor unions had been formed to demand better working conditions and pay increases for their workers. But these unions did not allow blacks to join. Philip was frustrated because few people seemed interested in helping black workers. In 1925, he decided to help these workers by forming the Brotherhood of Sleeping Car Porters, a union for the employees of the Pullman Railroad Company. It was ten years before the porters' union won the fight for better wages and working conditions. When the railroad company finally agreed to their terms, the union named Philip "Saint Philip of the Pullman Porters." With the Pullman victory, Philip became famous.

Personality Profile

Career: Labor and civil rights leader.

Born: April 15, 1889, in Crescent City, Florida, to James and Elizabeth Randolph.

Died: May 16, 1979.

Education: Cookman Institute; City College of New York.

Awards: Honorary LL.D., Howard University, 1941; Spingarn Medal, NAACP, 1942; civil rights award, American Federation of Teachers, 1973.

In those days there were separate units for blacks and whites in the military. Philip began organizing a huge protest march in Washington, D.C., calling for an end to segregation in the U.S. armed forces and the defense industry. He told President Roosevelt that 100,000 blacks would march in the demonstration, and the president tried to persuade Philip to stop the protest. Philip was polite but determined. When it became obvious that he would not call off the protest, President Roosevelt issued Executive Order 8802 which made racial discrimination illegal in the defense industry. After the order was issued, Philip agreed to cancel the march.

Philip kept fighting for racial justice. By 1948, the U.S. Army was desegregated, and, in the 1950s, the labor unions finally allowed black workers to join them. Philip also remained active throughout the civil rights movement of the 1960s. Martin Luther King, Jr. referred to him as the Chief, and it was Philip who began organizing the 1963 March on Washington. Over 250,000 people participated in the demonstration for jobs and freedom. Philip continued as president of the Brotherhood of Sleeping Car Porters until he was seventy-nine. He died in 1979 at the age of ninety.

Accomplishments

1917 Edited *The Hotel Messenger.*

1925 Organized the Brotherhood of Sleeping Car Porters.

1940-41 Lobbied the government to desegregate the defense industry and organized a protest march on Washington, D.C.

1957 Elected vice-president of the American Federation of Labor and the Congress of Industrial Organizations.

1963 Organized the March on Washington.

Bayard Rustin

B ayard's family didn't have very much money, but they had food on their table. It was actually leftovers from banquets his grandfather catered. There were plenty of special party foods in the fridge, but the rest of the cupboards were usually bare.

Bayard was an honor student and a member of the choir, debating society, tennis, and football teams.

Bayard was an honor student and a member of the choir, debating society, tennis, and football teams. He graduated in 1928, but his family did not have enough money to send him to university. He held a variety of jobs, including singing in a Greenwich Village café in New York City. At this time, Greenwich Village was an area where African Americans and open-minded whites met and discussed ways of obtaining civil rights for blacks. At twenty-six, Bayard joined the Young Communist League because he felt they were pushing for civil rights. Two years later, he became a league organizer.

Gradually Bayard became upset with the Communists. He felt they were more interested in achieving political power than in civil rights. By 1941, Bayard felt his beliefs were no longer the same as those of the Communists, and he left the party. He joined the Fellowship of Reconciliation because he felt the group wanted to achieve the same things that he did. The Fellowship was a religious group that wanted to find peaceful solutions to world problems.

During World War II, Bayard was drafted into the army. He did not believe in violence and could not bring himself to kill another person, even if it was in the midst of a world war. In 1943, he was jailed because he refused to join the army. Bayard was released two-and-a-half years later. The time in jail did not change him. He still believed in peaceful solutions to world problems and wanted to fight for civil rights.

Bayard was also arrested during protest rallies in the South. He helped found the Congress of Racial Equality (CORE). In 1947, CORE organized the historic "journey of reconciliation." This took the form of bus rides in which African Americans and liberal whites drove across the southern states to gather support for civil rights. These bus rides became known as The Freedom Rides. Bayard was jailed for twenty-two days during the rides.

Personality Profile

Career: Civil rights leader and executive director of the A. Philip Randolph Institute.

Born: March 17, 1910, in West Chester, Pennsylvania, to Janifer and Julia Rustin.

Died: August 24, 1987, in New York City.

Education: West Chester High School, Cheney State Teachers College, Wilberforce University, and City College of New York.

Awards: Man of the Year, Pittsburgh chapter of the NAACP, 1965; Eleanor Roosevelt Award, Trade Union Conference of Pittsburg, 1965; and Stephen Wise Award, American Jewish Congress, 1981.

Bayard's interest in civil rights led him to Martin Luther King, Jr., one of the movement's most prominent leaders. The two strongly believed in nonviolent means to achieve civil rights. Bayard helped Martin plan the bus boycott in Montgomery, Alabama, which ended assigned seating for blacks and whites on the bus. After this success, Bayard, Martin, and others wanted to continue the struggle for civil rights. In 1957, they formed the Southern Christian Leadership Conference to stage protests and rallies across the South. Martin was elected president, while Bayard was named his special assistant.

In 1963, Bayard helped coordinate the March on Washington, the largest demonstration of the civil rights movement. More than 250,000 people marched on the nation's capital to mark the 100th anniversary of the ending of slavery.

When he was fifty-five, Bayard became director of the A. Philip Randolph Institute in New York City. The Institute is an educational, civil rights, and labor organization. Bayard remained director until his death on August 24, 1987, of a heart attack.

Accomplishments

1938 Moved to Harlem, New York, to become a Young Communist League organizer.

1941 Resigned from the Young Communist League and joined the Fellowship of Reconciliation.

1942 Co-founded the Congress of Racial Equality.

1963 Co-organizer of the March on Washington.

1964 Appointed director of the A. Philip Randolph Institute.

Index

1 2 3 4 5 6 7 8 9 0 Printed in Canada 4 3 2 1 0 9 8 7 6 5